SOCIALIST HISTO

SOCIALIST HISTORY
OCCASIONAL PUBLICATION
No. 32

THE REAL HISTORY OF CHARTISM
OR
EIGHT FALLACIES ABOUT THE CHARTIST MOVEMENT

DAVID GOODWAY

2013

Published by the Socialist History Society 2013
978-0-9555138-8-6
Designed and typeset by SHS 2013

Acknowledgement

The Socialist History Society wishes to thank the Bishopsgate Institute in London for permission to use illustrations from its unique archive and for hosting the public meeting on 19 April 2012 which led to this Occasional Publication.

For details of all Socialist History Society events:
www.socialisthistorysociety.co.uk

The Six Points of the People's Charter.

1. A VOTE for every man twenty-one years of age, of sound mind, and not undergoing punishment for crime.

2. THE BALLOT.—To protect the elector in the exercise of his vote.

3. NO PROPERTY QUALIFICATION for Members of Parliament—thus enabling the constituencies to return the man of their choice, be he rich or poor.

4. PAYMENT OF MEMBERS, thus enabling an honest tradesman, working man, or other person, to serve a constituency, when taken from his business to attend to the interests of the country.

5. EQUAL CONSTITUENCIES, securing the same amount of representation for the same number of electors, instead of allowing small constituencies to swamp the votes of large ones.

6. ANNUAL PARLIAMENTS, thus presenting the most effectual check to bribery and intimidation, since though a constituency might be bought once in seven years (even with the ballot), no purse could buy a constituency (under a system of universal suffrage) in each ensuing twelvemonth; and since members, when elected for a year only, would not be able to defy and betray their constituents as now.

Subjoined are the names of the gentlemen who embodied these principles into the document called the "People's Charter," at an influential meeting held at the British Coffee House, London, on the 7th of June, 1837:—

Daniel O'Connell, Esq., M.P.,
John Arthur Roebuck, Esq., M.P.
John Temple Leader, Esq., M.P.
Charles Hindley, Esq., M.P.
Thomas Perronet Thompson, Esq., M.P.
William Sharman Crawford, Esq., M.P.

Mr. Henry Hetherington.
Mr. John Cleave.
Mr. James Watson.
Mr. Richard Moore.
Mr. William Lovett.
Mr. Henry Vincent.

W. COLLINS, PRINTER, "WEEKLY TIMES" OFFICE, DUDLEY.

Contents

Preface

In 2012, the Socialist History Society held a series of talks at Bishopsgate Institute on 'Aspects of Popular Protest'. They were conceived in part as a response to the outbreak of mass rioting that occurred first in London and then rapidly spread to several towns and cities across the country in early August 2011. The SHS decided that it might be able to make a small contribution to a wider public understanding of the nature of public protest by examining some key aspects of the history of political protest movements over past centuries, including those that were committed to radical reform like Chartism and others campaigning for popular justice at various levels, such as Luddism.

The major outbreak of public unrest in contemporary Britain in August 2011 was initially sparked by the fatal shooting of Mark Duggan by police in Tottenham. The public anger rapidly spiralled out of control into major public disorder with thousands of people involved in looting, arson and civil unrest. More than three thousand people were eventually arrested and over a thousand were charged with various public order offences, many receiving punitive sentences as magistrates sought to make an example of the rioters. Politicians and social commentators engaged in much anxious debates in the media about the causes of the riots. The talks on popular protest were the SHS's way of engaging with these discussions.

Clearly, these riots had many political, social and economic ramifications, but they also seemed to lack any precise political ambitions beyond an expression of anger and, while the events demonstrated a profound sense of alienation among large swathes of the population, particularly the inner city youth, they did not constitute the emergence of a new political movement in any shape or form.

The vast differences and possible parallels between these 21st Century disturbances, which quickly became branded as the 'Facebook riots', and the incidences of popular protest in previous centuries were issues well worth subjecting to close scrutiny.

As part of the SHS's series of talks, social historian David Goodway, an authority on the Chartists and a long-term member of the SHS, delivered a talk in the library of Bishopsgate Institute on Chartism as a mass protest movement of the working class. The presentation was extremely well received by a full house and has now resulted in this SHS Occasional Publication.

Other talks in this series covered new research on "Captain Swing" by Dr Carl Griffin and the post-Second World War squatters' campaigns by Paul Burnham.

In Occasional Publication 32, Dr Goodway reminds us that Chartism was an extensive and popular national political movement of the working class unlike any that had occurred in history. Indeed, Goodway claims that it is "the highpoint of the British working-class movement" and as such it is constantly worth re-examining in all its complexity.

The Socialist History Society believes that this study by David Goodway provides both a succinct and readable introduction to this important mass movement and offers a useful overview of the many historiographical approaches that have taken Chartism as their focus of attention in recent years. We are pleased to be able to make it available in print and believe that it deserves to be widely read.

David Morgan on behalf of the editors
July 2013

The Presentation of the Chartist Petition by Mr Feargus O'Connor 1848

The Real History of Chartism
or Eight Fallacies about the Chartist Movement

Introduction

Thank you so much for asking me to talk to the Socialist History Society tonight. I had wondered, though, why the invitation hadn't come substantially earlier, since I am a long-time member of the Society and before that subscribed to *Our History* for many years.

I should like indeed to express my intellectual indebtedness to the Communist Party of Great Britain and, especially, to its Historians' Group. I would emphasise that Communist politics have never had any attraction for me; but I admired – and continue to admire – British Communists for their interest in culture, both elite and popular, and the historians as exemplars of historical materialism (and I do consider myself to be an historical materialist). I have recently been looking through copies of *Marxism Today* which I bought in the mid-1960s – there is, for example, an impressive evaluation of Kipling's literary achievement – and this has led me to appreciate the extent to which the Communist Party tradition has shaped my historical outlook.[1]

During 1964-5 I read Edward Thompson's great *William Morris: Romantic to Revolutionary* (in its first, Lawrence & Wishart edition) and Eric Hobsbawm's wonderful collection of articles, *Labouring Men*, two of the books I most esteem, as well as Dona Torr's *Tom Mann and His Times*. Is there anybody else who will acknowledge the impact on them of Torr's biography, especially its Part III, the background chapters written up by Christopher Hill and A L Morton? I also recall the intense excitement with which I bought in my final summer at Oxford a second-hand copy of *Democracy and the Labour Movement*, the volume edited by John Saville in honour of Dona Torr, with its seminal essays by Hill and Hobsbawm. And in 1965 I escaped from Oxford to become a full-time research student of Eric Hobsbawm in London.

Retrospectively it seems strange that Edward Thompson was not a member of the Historians' Group – yet in the 1950s he saw himself as a poet and was affiliated to the Writers' Group - and it was his wife Dorothy who made occasional forays from Yorkshire to attend meetings of the Historians. Dorothy Thompson died in January 2011 and six months later I participated in a round-table discussion on her 'legacy for Chartist Studies'. In preparation I read for the first time from cover to cover the edition she had given me of her book *The Chartists* (1984).

I was very struck by her rejection of the major interpretations of Chartism, what we may call the Whig or Fabian and the Marxist:

> To Whiggish historians, watching the inevitable unfolding of British democratic institutions, the Chartists were premature. By trying to bring within the pale of the constitution the uneducated, the Irish, the women of the lower orders, they were anticipating a degree of participation in the processes of representative government which would only be possible after a further three-quarters of a century of education and instruction. Had the policies of the LWMA (London Working Men's Association) in its earliest days been followed, this argument implies, the better sections of the lower classes – the educated and rational – might have been admitted to the franchise well before 1867. Only the behaviour of the undisciplined mob, under the influence of unscrupulous demagogues, frightened those men of goodwill among the powerful who would otherwise have followed the course of history by promoting the gradual admission to participation of those who had shown themselves to be worthy of it. This view had its exponents during the Chartist years...and it underlies the view of Chartism which sees the failure of Lovett's attempts at leadership as the chief reason for the movement's lack of success. Mark Hovell certainly held it...

The contrasting 'framework' is 'suggested by the view of history which sees it as developing towards a classless socialist society':

> Those aspects of the Chartist movement which were based on the defence of 'artisan values' – the independence of the craftsman, his control over his personal environment, the defence of craft standards [all central to Chartist thinking, DG] – or the desire felt by many factory workers to leave the industrial districts and join communities of rural or semi-rural producers, are seen as backward-looking, peasant-inspired, and often blamed on the Irish origins of Feargus O'Connor. In this socialist teleology, many of the most highly-charged and powerful impulses behind the protests of the common people are seen as manifestations of 'false consciousness'. The failure of the movement lay in the inability of its leaders to transform the energy of protest into a genuinely revolutionary consciousness which would have made possible the transfer of class power and the overthrow of the capitalist system.[2]

It seemed to me that in opposition to these two interpretations Dorothy Thompson was considering Chartism 'on its own terms', seeing it in the way that it perceived itself. I am aware of the problems attached to and the limitations of this approach, but I applaud her attempt to rescue what John Saville called 'the greatest popular movement of modern Britain' and again 'the greatest of all mass movements of the past two centuries' from 'the enormous condescension of posterity'.[3]

Until the late twentieth-century Chartism had been damned or ridiculed by its (class) enemies and criticised as lacking in some way - or ways – by most left (usually Marxist) historians. Largely under Dorothy Thompson's inspiration a new school of Chartist historiography emerged, seeing Chartism 'on its own terms'. This is what I am referring to, very clumsily I realise, when I speak of 'the real history of Chartism'.

Looking back, I can appreciate that my own work on London, which was finally completed as a PhD thesis in 1979 and then rapidly published as *London Chartism, 1838-1848* in 1982, belongs to this new approach. But although I had known Dorothy since the late 1960s and had heard her speak on several occasions, I definitely was not influenced by her at this time. Her publications on Chartism were exceedingly sparse and slight, with the exception of her valuable collection of documents, *The Early Chartists* (1971), until the appearance as late as 1984 of *The Chartists*. This book, by the way, is a series of studies of Chartism, not a narrative history. The year before she had edited *The Chartist Experience: Studies in Working-Class Radicalism and Culture, 1830-60* with her former doctoral student, James Epstein. Also in 1983 Jim Epstein brought out his impressive study of Feargus O'Connor's early political career, *The Lion of Freedom: Feargus O'Connor and the Chartist Movement, 1832-1842*, which I am inclined to view as Dorothy's best book so infused is it with her ideas and perspectives.

One can now see that the interpretative stance of these publications of 1982-4 was anticipated by A R Schoyen's magnificent biography of George Julian Harney, *The Chartist Challenge* (1958), as well as many articles and introductions by John Saville, culminating in his *1848: The British State and the Chartist Movement* (1987).[4] The best of the contributions in *Chartist Studies*, the uneven collection edited by Asa Briggs in 1959, also belong here - I am thinking particularly of the chapters contributed by JFC Harrison as well as Briggs's own. In addition, it is worth mentioning at this point a very different study - from the top: F C Mather's *Public Order in the Age of the Chartists* (1959), which I know John Saville, like myself, valued.

Many of the historians involved in the new school of Chartist historiography since 1982-4 were students of Dorothy Thompson at the University of Birmingham.[5] The two major contributors, though, were not. Paul A Pickering's *Chartism and the Chartists in Manchester and Salford* (1995) is one of the finest regional studies; and his *Feargus O'Connor: A Political Life* (2008) is the first acceptable full biography, although still surprisingly short. Most important of all is Malcolm Chase's *Chartism: A New History* (2007), a masterly narrative history which at last supplants Mark Hovell's ancient *The Chartist Movement*, unfinished when the author was killed in the First World War, and completed by the medievalist T.F. Tout for its publication in 1918, and which has been responsible for so many misconceptions.

Consideration of Chartism is certainly bedevilled with misconceptions and outright error. Almost all traditional assessments – the *bien-pensant* judgments that find their ways into general histories of the period – are to be rejected. I have here chosen to explore only eight fallacies about the movement for want of more time, yet the list seems endless. I pondered over whether to include the characterisation of the Kennington Common demonstration of 10 April 1848 as a 'fiasco', of 1848 as a year of little activity, of occupational support as skewed towards dying trades, not factory workers, and of the supposed lack of participation in the movement of trade unionists and their societies, but have decided on the following. I would be much surprised if at least one of these was not subscribed to by each of those present this evening.

(1) It was the London Working Men's Association (LWMA) which brought the movement into being.
(2) The division between the advocates of moral force and of physical force fatally undermined the movement.
(3) Chartism never took off in London.
(4) The Land Plan was a reactionary, irrelevant diversion.
(5) Feargus O'Connor was a buffoonish demagogue and altogether a disaster.
(6) Chartism was in some fundamental way socialist.
(7) Without Chartism there would have been no Labour Party.
(8) Geographically, Chartism was a movement of the industrial North and Midlands.

My sixth fallacy is likely to be the killer for members of the Socialist History Society. The crudest version of the eighth would confine Chartism to the North; in its more sophisticated, but unusual, form it will include the Midlands as well.

1. It was the London Working Men's Association (LWMA) which brought the movement into being

In May 1838 the LWMA, the secretary of which was William Lovett, published *The People's Charter*, which took the form of a parliamentary bill for what soon became known as 'the Six Points': universal male suffrage, equal electoral districts, voting by secret ballot, no property qualification for MPs, payment of members and annual parliaments. There was nothing new about this programme. Its demands had been voiced by the movements for parliamentary reform reaching back to the late eighteenth century. That for equal electoral districts (equality, by the way, in terms of population not area) was the only point not advocated by Major Cartwright as long before as 1776 in *Take Your Choice*. What was different in 1838 was the newly formed working class and the acute distress to which it was subjected by the current downturn of the trade cycle, coupled with the rousing of the North of England first by the Factory Movement and then by the quasi-insurrectionary Anti-Poor Law Movement into which it had passed.

In 1837 the Birmingham Political Union (BPU) had been revived. First formed in 1829, by 1832 it had become the strongest and most influential radical organisation the country. The BPU, though, was very different from the other principal constituents of Chartism in that its leadership was solidly middle class, the outstanding figure being the banker Thomas Attwood whose principal panacea for the nation's ills was currency reform. The BPU began drafting a National Petition which, on its completion, also in May 1838, contained all Six Points of the Charter. The juncture between London and Birmingham occurred the same month at a great demonstration in Glasgow, where Attwood proposed that a National Convention should be summoned. By the time the Charter was officially launched at a meeting in Birmingham in August, mass support for the new movement was already being mobilised, particularly in Lancashire and Yorkshire.

So the third area to contribute significantly to emergent Chartism was the North of England. There Feargus O'Connor was establishing himself as the dominant leader – as he was shortly to become of the national movement for almost ten years. O'Connor was an Irish gentleman who had sat as MP for Co. Cork from 1832 until he was unseated after the general election of 1835 for lack of the property qualification: his annual income was less than £600 from landed property. He acquired his position in British radical politics to a considerable extent through his proprietorship of the impressive weekly newspaper, the *Northern Star and Leeds General Advertiser*, which had begun to appear in November 1837.

In the late summer and early autumn of 1838 'monster meetings' were held throughout the country to adopt the Charter and elect delegates to sit in the forthcoming Convention. A total of 200,000 were said to be present at the Birmingham meeting in August; 300,000 at Kersall Moor, Manchester; 250,000 at the West Riding demonstration at Peep Green; 30,000 even at the Western Counties demonstration on Trowle Common (between Trowbridge and Bradford-on-Avon). In contrast, London's Palace Yard meeting was attended by no more than 30,000 and probably more likely 15,000. Not only were signatures collected for the Petition, but a 'Rent' was raised for the maintenance of the delegates and for the work of the Convention.

The LWMA had certainly published *The People's Charter*, but had otherwise little or nothing to do with the mass mobilisation of 1838. As Harney was to observe fifty years later:

> ... the London Working Men's Association and the Birmingham Political Union combined could never have produced a tremendous uprising as the Chartist movement became in consequence of another contributory force, that of the impassioned masses of Lancashire, Cheshire, and Yorkshire, to which should be added those of Northumberland, Durham, and, in Cumberland, Carlisle and its neighbourhood. The cruel evils inflicted by the unreformed factory system, and the inhumanity with which the New Poor Law was introduced, had goaded the masses of the first three named counties especially, well nigh to desperation. And when the flame of combustible mass was fanned by such a preacher as Rev. J. R. Stephens (to say nothing of Richard Oastler, Feargus O'Connor, and others), the present day reader may have some faint idea of the kind of movement which set aside the [academical] teachings of the London Working Men's Association and the stereotyped political guidance of the Birmingham Council.[6]

2. The division between the advocates of moral force and of physical force fatally undermined the movement

This seems to me mainly a non-issue. Obviously Chartism's mode of action was a problem. In each of three years a National Petition was presented to Parliament; and the question was therefore 'What was to be done, if it were rejected?' But the mainstream Chartist response to this problem was always 'Peaceably if we can, forcibly if we must'.

Twice – in 1839-40 and 1848 – there was the resort to force with attempted risings. There can be doubt that Britain was on the brink of a widespread insurrection during 1839. The planned 'Sacred Month'- that is, a general strike - of summer 1839, however, was to be abandoned for lack of support. And then, when in 1842, a strike movement (entirely independent of the national leadership but with extensive local Chartist involvement and forethought) did break out, the leadership almost without exception rejected it.[7]

The alienation after the Newport Rising of respectable middle-class radical sympathisers, scared off by the 'terrible "raw head and bloody bones"' which now characterised Chartism, as it became (we are now able to see) a typical movement of the oppressed, mobilising around martyrs and prisoners and support for their dependants, probably did weaken it.[8] Yet the loss of the LWMA and Lovett was insignificant in impact.[9]

3. Chartism never took off in London

London did fail the movement in the first phase, 1838-9. It was inexplicably 'apathetic'. But from 1840 it became a major Chartist centre. This was recognised by the removal there of the Chartist Executive from

Manchester in 1843. The *Northern Star* followed, relocating from Leeds in 1844 and changing its title to the *Northern Star and National Trades' Journal.*[10]

4. The Land Plan was a reactionary, irrelevant diversion

Five full years intervened between 1842 and the final revival of Chartism. An ideal means for consolidating (and indeed extending) the much diminished movement was achieved when the Chartist Land Co-Operative Society was launched in 1845. This scheme, undeniably O'Connor's brainchild, offered its members the possibility of acquiring agricultural smallholdings.

Shares cost £1 6s (£1.30) each and could be paid for in instalments. Two shares entitled the holder to enter a ballot for a two-acre holding, three for three acres and four for four acres (the largest holding). When an estate was bought, it was divided into holdings in proportion to the paid-up membership of each class, the ballot for each being taken separately. Each successful shareholder would, in addition to the land, receive a newly built, specially designed cottage and an advance of money as initial capital to help with seed, stock and the like.

The Land Plan collapsed, 1848-51, through a legal shortcoming: it was not registered as a joint stock company (this would have been much too expensive, requiring a special Act of Parliament) but neither was it accepted as a friendly society – because it wasn't one. The first colony had opened in the south-east at Herringsgate (O'Connorville), near Rickmansworth. It was the Minster Lovell estate, near Witney, Oxfordshire, that became Charterville. The other three colonies were close to Charterville in Gloucestershire and Worcestershire. A mere 250 members were settled on the land; but the total number of shareholders was in the order of 70,000. O'Connor had touched a deep longing in the British people and he himself was staggered by the response to his lottery. The industrial areas and the agricultural districts, for the first time responding significantly to Chartism, were equally enthusiastic – at least about the Land Company.

A thoroughgoing reassessment of the Land Plan has been undertaken in recent decades and the new school of Chartist historiography displays much sympathy, even empathy, for it. There are three principal grounds for this remarkable reversal of opinion.

First, it is now appreciated that the basic principles and aims of the Land Company were by no means unrealistic or impracticable. At fault were its specific organisation and its management by O'Connor. John Saville came to believe that the small farm was not an economic impossibility in the second half of the nineteenth century. Anything less than four acres, he considered, was probably too small for a reasonable living in most parts of Britain (and, of course, there were two- and three-acre holdings under the Land Plan). But 'an intelligent man, helped by a good family', said Saville, could, and did, make a living on four acres in any of the Chartist colonies – and in some cases success was attained with less.[11] None other than John Stuart Mill judged the Land Plan as 'well-conceived':

> There is at present an experiment in progress, in more than one part of England, for the creation of peasant proprietors. The project is of Chartist origin, and its first colony is now in full operation near Rickmansworth, in Hertfordshire....The originator of this experiment appears to have successfully repelled (before a tribunal by no means prepossessed in his favour, a Committee of the House of Commons) the imputations which were lavished upon his project, and upon his mode of executing it. Should its issue ultimately be unfavourable, the cause of failure will be in the details of management, not in the Principle.

This passage was included in the 1848 and 1849 editions of Mill's *Principles of Political Economy*, but was altered in the third edition of 1852.[12]

Secondly, the land was a central issue in nineteenth-century British radical thought, not only before but also after Chartism. It was omnipresent, not solely a possession of O'Connor's 'strange mind'.[13] During the 1840s the Chartist Land Company was just one of a fairly large number of societies and movements which aimed at securing land for members of the working class. For example, the National Association of United Trades for the Employment of Labour in Agriculture and Manufactures was set up in 1845 as the companion organisation of the important National Association of United Trades for the Protection of Labour, a Chartist aligned federation of trade societies. The previous year the famous Rochdale Pioneers, whose innovation of the dividend was to transform co-operative retailing, were as Owenite in inspiration and aspiration as their predecessors, including among their objectives that 'as a further benefit and security to the members...the Society shall purchase or rent an *estate or estates of land*, which shall be cultivated by members who may be out of employment, or whose labour may be badly remunerated'.[14]

Thirdly, the reassessment of the Land Plan has been concurrent with a re-evaluation of its creator, O'Connor, both now being viewed 'on their own terms'.

5. Feargus O'Connor was a buffoonish demagogue and altogether a disaster

Jim Epstein, who describes O'Connor as 'an agitator of extraordinary abilities', puts the case for him eloquently:

> O'Connor's popularity was based upon his unrivalled talents as an agitator, his brilliance as an orator, his indefatigable energy in the

> radical cause; but his standing within the ranks of Chartism was also founded upon the consistent and intelligent leadership which he had provided since the mid-1830s, his insistent class perspective and class tone, his emphasis upon the need to establish permanent organisations of independent working-class political struggle. He came to symbolise the independence of working-class radicalism. Certain aspects of his style of leadership, particularly its highly personalised character, may appear unattractive and may have proved detrimental to the cause which he so passionately espoused. However, his leadership style must be judged not against some modern model of revolutionary leadership, but within its own historical context. Nor should the paternalistic tone which he occasionally adopted obscure the essential democratic spirit which infused both his own and other Chartists' politics.[15]

So O'Connor was a member of the Executive of the National Charter Association, but this was always as a result of being elected to it. We should take note of Epstein's insistence on the necessity of judging his leadership 'within its own historical context', another way of saying 'on its own terms'.

From 1846 there is a revealing analysis by Harney, then editor of the *Northern Star*, in a letter to Engels, the close friendship between the two young men dating from 1843. We do not have the letter to which Harney was replying, but clearly Engels had been urging his friend to elbow O'Connor out of the Chartist leadership.

> I must next notice what you say about my "*leadership*". First let me remark that you are too hard upon O'Connor....I must do O'C. the justice to say that he never interferes with what I write in the paper nor does he know what I write until he sees the paper. You have thought proper in the letter I am now commenting on to credit me with all the revolutionary virtues. You say I am "international", "revolutionary", "energetical", "proletarian", "more of a Frenchman than an Englishman", "Atheistical, Republican and Communist". I am too old a soldier to blush at this accumulation of virtues credited to my account, but supposing it to be even as you say, it does not follow that I am qualified for "leadership". A popular chief should be possessed of magnificent bodily appearance, an iron frame, eloquence, or at least a ready fluency of tongue. I have none of these. O'C. has them all – at least in degree. A popular leader should possess great animal courage, contempt of pain and death, and be not altogether ignorant of arms and military science. No chief or leader that has hitherto appeared in the English movement has these qualifications. We have never had a Barbès, for instance. In these qualifications I am decidedly deficient. I know nothing of arms, have no stomach for fighting, and would rather die after some other fashion than by bullet or rope. From a knowledge of myself and all the men who do live and figure in the Chartist movement, I am convinced that even in this

> respect, was O'C. thrown overboard, we might go further and fare worse.

Harney commented astutely that 'the very qualities you give me the credit of possessing, and which you emphatically sum up in the sentence, "You are the *only* Englishman who is really free of *all* prejudices that distinguish the Englishman from the Continental man", are sufficient of themselves to prevent my being a leader': 'If I am "the *only* Englishman, &c", it follows that I would be a chief without an army, a leader without followers'. Harney, a Londoner and indeed a proletarian, was then insufficiently English in outlook, whereas O'Connor, who belonged to the Irish gentry, exerted a mesmeric appeal on the English working class, many of whom were, of course, either Irish-born or of Irish origin.[16]

These differences resulted in O'Connor sacking Harney from the *Northern Star* in 1850. Yet Harney continued to hold O'Connor in affectionate regard. Here is a vignette recollected in his last years:

> The coach arrives, and 'There he is!' is the cry. As the coach halts, a traveller, stalwart, large-limbed, fair, freckled, auburn-haired (his enemies call him 'red-headed'), in the very prime of his life, of a commanding presence and gifted with a sonorous voice, with graceful bows and smiles, makes his acknowledgments. Responding to the cheers of the weavers, he exhorts them to 'stand by the Charter, and no surrender'. Then the coach is borne onward to its destination: the parting cheers of the weavers ringing sweet music in the ears of Feargus O'Connor.[17]

Edward Aveling, who already knew Harney as a member of the Marx-Engels family circle, interviewed him at his small house in Richmond, Surrey, a few months before his death and listed the many portraits decorating the living room: of Marx and Engels and, from the Chartist years, Richard Oastler, Joseph Rayner Stephens, William Lovett (rather surprisingly given their antagonism during the late 1830s), John Frost and naturally O'Connor.[18]

6. Chartism was in some fundamental way socialist

In the final decade of the movement (that is to say, *after* 1848) the remnants of Chartism did move strongly towards socialism; and not only Harney but also Ernest Jones became close to Engels and Marx. But in its heyday Chartism was in no way socialist. How could it have been with its enthusiasm for peasant proprietorship?

After Edward Thompson's death in 1993, I came to know Dorothy very well and would stay with her in Worcester when driving from Yorkshire to the south-west. I was startled when she - an eager reader of Palme Dutt's *Labour Monthly* as a schoolgirl after she had joined the Communist Party aged fifteen - remarked around 2000, 'I think I've become a Liberal, a Tom Paine Liberal'. The more I pondered over this statement the more I thought that I, a libertarian with a contempt for the politicians of the Labour Party, also had considerable sympathy for Paineite Liberalism. The two great ideological forebears of the Chartists were William Cobbett and Tom Paine. 'Mr Thomas Paine, if you please. I will not suffer the memory of that great man to be so traduced'. I cite from memory, a report almost certainly in the *Northern Star* of a meeting in some Chartist locality, in which another member had innocently spoken of 'Tom Paine'.

When I last saw Dorothy Thompson in August 2010, she informed me happily that she had voted Liberal Democrat in the general election of May. At that stage she was content with the policies of the coalition government, but I know she would have profoundly abhorred the austerity programme as it was to emerge. But here we have Dorothy Thompson, the pioneer of the interpretation of Chartism 'on its own terms', finally coming personally to adhere to the politics of Chartism. For, although there was a minority Tory Radical current, Chartists were essentially Liberal. As Malcolm Chase observes: '...most Chartists who lived long enough... supported the Liberal Party in old age...'[19]

There is a well-known report of a meeting in Halifax in 1885 to commemorate the passage of the Third Reform Act the preceding year:

> Twenty-two members of the old Chartist Association...met at Maude's Temperance Hotel to spend a Social Evening in celebration of the incorporation in the law of the land of the principal portion of the Charter. The chair was occupied by Mr John Culpan, who was secretary when Mr Ernest Jones was a candidate for Halifax in 1847, and also all the time Mr Jones was in prison for advocating measures which have now a place on the statute book.... Mr Joseph Foreman... moved – 'That the best thanks of this meeting be given to Mr Gladstone and his government for passing into law those principles which we have endeavoured during a long life to enjoy'.... Mr B. Wilson moved, and Mr Shackleton seconded, a vote of thanks to the two Liberal members who have given Mr Gladstone and his government continuous support. This was also cordially adopted, the company rising to their feet. The ages of those present averaged upwards of 65 years, and varied from 62 to 76.[20]

7. Without Chartism there would have been no Labour Party

Chartism was the culmination of half-a-century of political radicalism: of the artisan Jacobinism initiated in the 1790s. Yet its relationship to later radicalism was entirely different. A profound hiatus exists around the mid-century. Chartism and former Chartists could not fail to influence developments in trade unionism and the renewed movement for parliamentary reform of the 1860s. But the fierce class consciousness and determination to maintain an independent class position were lost. The latter was only retrieved by the Labour Party, founded in 1900, as late as 1918. There was no real continuity between Chartism and the Labour Party, whether ideological let alone (to any significant extent) in personnel.[21]

People, especially students writing essays, want movements to be successful, to be able to trace a path of progress over the years, and are unable to cope with historical failures. Chartism however was defeated, achieving nothing while it still existed. Although the property qualification for MPs was abolished in 1858, this reform owed nothing to Chartist pressure. This great movement indeed was defeated so badly that, from the 1850s, demoralisation, emigration and the suppression of its memory ensued.

On the other hand, for me Chartism is the highpoint of the British working-class movement. Everything that follows is anti-climactic. The title of Theodore Rothstein's insightful study of 1929, *From Chartism to Labourism*, epitomises the descent admirably.

8. Geographically, Chartism was a movement of the industrial North and Midlands

While Chartism was generated – as a mass movement – by the industrial districts of both the North and the Midlands, its historical importance is that it was a national movement. It was the first nationally organised political movement of the working class to exist anywhere in the world. In this respect the National Charter Association (NCA), established in 1840, was crucial.

Jim Epstein has provided a very rough, but invaluable, guide to Chartist membership throughout the country over a crucial two-year period, autumn 1840 to autumn 1842, on the basis of the number of new NCA membership cards distributed to each locality. The largest memberships are shown as:

London	8,000
Manchester and Salford	3,300
Leicester	3,100
Sheffield	2,000
Bradford	1,500 – 1,900
Nottingham	1,650
Leeds	1,325
Merthyr Tydfil	1,100
Birmingham	1,000 – 1,200
Hanley (including Shelton)	1,100
Newcastle-upon-Tyne	1,000
Bilston	1,000

Unfortunately Epstein did not go further and, taking into account populations, calculate indices of participation. All the same, these figures delineate the Chartist heartlands: the hosiery districts of the East Midlands (Leicester and Nottingham), Sheffield, the woollen area of the West Riding (Leeds and Bradford, Halifax and Huddersfield), Manchester and its satellite towns (Stockport, Oldham, Ashton-under-Lyne, Rochdale, Bolton etc), the Potteries (Hanley, Shelton etc), the Black Country (Bilston etc) – all from the industrial North and Midlands – but with London, admittedly a huge city of almost two million, having the greatest absolute number of Chartists. Epstein points out that 'one of the most impressive features...was the widespread support for the NCA throughout the country...' Brighton and Bath both had 420 members, Gloucester 200 to 300, Cheltenham 270, Ipswich 120 to 140, and Salisbury 100.[22]

It is with that fact that I wish to conclude. Chartism was so extensive and popular, so national a movement, that even before the Land Plan, a southern cathedral city such as Salisbury, the primary inspiration the following decade of Anthony Trollope's somnolent 'Barchester', had a Chartist party of 100 members. In general, though, I trust I have made clear how very different the real history of Chartism, Chartism viewed on its own terms, is from the treatment of the movement in all the traditional accounts.

The Chartist Convention, John Street, Fitzroy Square, 1848
from *Illustrated London News*

Notes

1. Jack Dunman, 'Rudyard Kipling Re-Estimated', *Marxism Today*, IX, 8 (August 1965). Jack Dunman, 'Rudyard Kipling Re-Estimated: A Rejoinder', *Marxism Today*, X, 2 (February 1966), indicates, however, the degree of opposition his article had occasioned.
2. Dorothy Thompson, *The Chartists: Popular Politics in the Industrial Revolution* (New York: Pantheon Books, 1984), pp. 3-4.
3. John Saville, 'Introduction: R.G. Gammage and the Chartist Movement', to R.G. Gammage, *History of the Chartist Movement, 1837-1854* (1894; New York: Augustus M. Kelley, 1969), pp. 40, 66.
4. For a review of Saville's Chartist writings, see Malcolm Chase, 'The Chartist Movement and 1848', in David Howell, Dianne Kirby and Kevin Morgan (eds), *John Saville: Commitment and History: Themes from the Life and Work of a Socialist Historian* (London: Lawrence & Wishart and Socialist History Society, 2011).
5. For her students, see Owen Ashton, Robert Fyson and Stephen Roberts (eds), *The Duty of Discontent: Essays for Dorothy Thompson* (London: Mansell, 1995).
6. George Julian Harney, 'The Tremendous Uprising', Part 1, *Newcastle Weekly Chronicle*, 22 December 1888, reprinted in David Black and Chris Ford, *1839: The Chartist Insurrection* (London: Unkant Publishers, 2012), p. 209.
7. See the important study by Mick Jenkins, *The General Strike of 1842* (London: Lawrence & Wishart, 1980).
8. The quotation comes from Matthew Fletcher, the Bury surgeon who had been a member of the Convention (Dorothy Thompson (ed.), *The Early Chartists* (London and Basingstoke: Macmillan, 1971), p. 27).
9. See David Goodway, *London Chartism, 1838-1848* (Cambridge: Cambridge University Press, 1982), pp. 38-42; David Goodway, 'William Lovett', *Oxford Dictionary of National Biography.*
10. For London: Goodway, *London Chartism*, esp. pp. 38-53, 59-60.
11. Saville, 'Introduction, pp. 59-60.
12. John Saville, 'Irishman and Chartist', *New Left Review*, no.9 (May-June 1961), p. 61; John Saville, 'The Chartist Land Plan', *Bulletin of the Society for the Study of Labour History*, no. 3 (Autumn 1961), p. 11.
13. Mark Hovell, *The Chartist Movement* (Manchester: Manchester University Press, 2nd edn, 1925), p. 272.
14. George Jacob Holyoake, *Self-Help by the People: The History of the Rochdale Pioneers, 1844-1892* (London: Allen & Unwin, 10th edn., 1918), p. 12.
15. James Epstein, *The Lion of Freedom: Feargus O'Connor and the Chartist Movement, 1832-1842* (London: Croom Helm, 1982), pp. 313-15.
16. Letter from Harney to Engels, 30 March 1846, in Frank Gees Black and Renee Métivier Black (eds), *The Harney Papers* (Assen: Van Gorcum, 1969), pp. 240-42.

17. *Newcastle Weekly Chronicle*, 20 February 1892.
18. Edward Aveling, 'George Julian Harney: A Straggler of 1848', *Social Democrat*, January 1897.
19. Malcolm Chase, *Chartism: A New History* (Manchester: Manchester University Press, 2007), p. 234. It was to Tory Radicalism that none other than Harney gravitated in old age (see George Julian Harney, *The Chartists Were Right: Selected Columns from the* Newcastle Weekly Chronicle, *1890-97*, ed David Goodway (Pontypool: Merlin Press, forthcoming)).
20. Cited by Benjamin Wilson, *The Struggles of an Old Chartist* (1887), reprinted in David Vincent (ed), *Testaments of Radicalism: Memoirs of Working Class Politicians 1790-1885* (London: Europa Publications, 1977), pp. 241-2.
21. But, for the opposite view, see Ian Bullock, 'Chartism Old and New', *Chartist*, no. 258 (September-October 2012).
22. Epstein, *Lion of Freedom*, pp. 230-32. The figures in *The Lion of Freedom* are derived from the more detailed Appendix C of James A. Epstein, 'Feargus O'Connor and the English Working-Class Radical Movement, 1832-1841: A Study in National Chartist Leadership' (Birmingham PhD thesis, 1977), pp. 539-44, which unlike the book includes Salisbury. Oddly, neither thesis nor book lists any Scottish centre, but few localities in Scotland seem to have affiliated to the NCA.

Part of the Procession - Sketched at Blackfriars Bridge, 1848
from *Illustrated London News*

Appendices

1. A Chronology of Chartism

1832	June	The Reform Bill passed into law.
	December	The first general election was held under new legislation.
1833	May	Proscription of a meeting at Coldbath Fields, London, called by the National Union of the Working Classes to propose the holding of a National Convention. In the resulting mêlée Constable Culley of the new Metropolitan Police was stabbed to death.
	August	Factory Act, setting up Factory Inspectorate.
1833, 1834		Irish Coercion Acts.
1834	February	Launch of the Grand National Consolidated Trade Union (GNCTU)
	March	Prosecution of the six Dorchester Labourers (the 'Tolpuddle Martyrs'). They were sentenced to seven years' transportation.
	July	Passage of the Poor Law Amendment Act: the New Poor Law.
	August	Dissolution of the GNCTU.
1835	September	Passage of the Municipal Corporations Act.
1836	April	Beginning of a major financial crisis
	May	The newspaper duty was reduced from 6d to 1d, ending the 'War of the Unstamped'
	June	Foundation of the London Working Men's Association (LWMA)
1837	January	Foundation of the East London Democratic Association.
		The Poor Law Commissioners turned their attention to the North of England, meeting with widespread resistance.
	All year	Formation of Anti-Poor Law Associations in Lancashire and Yorkshire.
	February	The LWMA held its first public meeting.
	April	Glasgow Cotton Spinners strike.
	May	Birmingham Political Union revived.
	May-June	Conferences were held between radical MPs and the LWMA about parliamentary reform.
	July	General election.
	November	The *Northern Star and Leeds General Advertiser* began publication.
		South Lancashire Anti-Poor Law Association established.

	December	Prosecution of leaders of the Glasgow Cotton Spinners Union results in sentences of seven years' transportation.
		The government, at the suggestion of Daniel O'Connell, set up an official enquiry into trade unions.
1838	May	The East London Democratic Association became the London Democratic Association.
		The People's Charter published in London.
		The National Petition published in Birmingham.
		Great Glasgow rally.
	June	The Great Northern Union founded in Leeds
		The Northern Political Union founded in Newcastle.
	August	Great Birmingham rally
	Late summer/ autumn	Election of delegates at mass meetings to the General Convention.
	September	Kersall Moor meeting, Manchester.
		Manchester Anti-Corn Law Association founded.
	October	Richard Oastler removed from political agitation with the demand for the payment of £2000.
	November	Rev. Joseph Rayner Stephens addressed open-air meeting at Hyde, Cheshire, for which he was later arrested and imprisoned.
	December	Calton Hill 'moral force' resolutions carried in Edinburgh.
1839	February	The General Convention of the Industrious Classes met in London.
	March	The Anti-Corn-Law League was launched as a national organisation.
	April	Major-General Sir Charles Napier appointed to the command of the northern district.
	April-May	Llanidloes riots.
	May	The Chartist Convention moved to Birmingham.
		Beginning of the Rebecca Riots.
	June	The National Petition presented to Parliament by Thomas Attwood and John Fielden.
	July	The Bull Ring Riots in Birmingham, leading to arrest of William Lovett and John Collins.
		Return of the Convention to London.
	12 July	The House of Commons rejected the Petition by 235 votes to 46.
	15 July	Convention called for the 'Sacred Month' to begin on 12 August.
	6 August	Call for Sacred Month rescinded.
	August	Passage of the Rural Police Act.
	September	Dissolution of the Convention .
	November	The Newport Rising.

	December	Publication of Thomas Carlyle's *Chartism*, raising the 'Condition of England Question'.
	Winter and spring	Extensive arrests of Chartists, both nationally and locally.
1840	9 January	John Frost found guilty of treason.
	11-12 Jan	Abortive risings in Sheffield and Dewsbury.
	19 Jan	Death sentence passed on Frost, Zephaniah Williams and William Jones.
	26-27 Jan	Abortive rising in Bradford.
	1 February	Sentences on Frost, Williams and Jones commuted to transportation for life.
	July	The National Charter Association (NCA) founded at a conference in Manchester.
	August	Daniel O'Connell founded the Loyal National Repeal Association.
	December	Oastler committed to the Fleet Prison.
1841	April	Foundation of the National Association of the United Kingdom for Promoting the Political and Social Improvement of the People by Lovett and his associates. O'Connor attacked Knowledge Chartism: 'the New Move'.
	August	General election, resulting in a Tory victory and Peel becoming prime minister.
	November	Joseph Sturge took up the suffrage question.
1842		A year of strikes, overwhelmingly resisting wage reductions, from its earliest months.
	April	Complete Suffrage Union Conference held in Birmingham. Chartist Convention met in London.
	May	House of Commons rejected the Second Chartist Petition by 287 votes to 49.
	July and August	Downturn of trade cycle reached its lowest point, leading to wage cuts, mass unemployment and unprecedented distress.
	August	A strike in Stalybridge, Cheshire, rapidly radiated to engulf the entire cotton spinning district, becoming a general strike for the People's Charter: the 'Plug Riots'. Yet repudiated by the Chartist leadership.
	December	Death of Dr John Taylor. Conference of Chartist and Complete Suffrage representatives at Birmingham, leading to the collapse of Complete Suffrage Union.
1843		Huge demonstrations held in Ireland by the Repeal Association. In October the government bans the final one, to be held at Clontarf.

	September	The Chartist Executive moved from Manchester to London.
1844	June	Factory Act, including adult females for the first time.
	November	The *Northern Star* moved from Leeds to London, becoming the *Northern Star and National Trades' Journal.*
	December	The Rochdale Society of Equitable Pioneers opened their Toad Lane store.
1845	March	Inauguration of the National Association of United Trades.
	April	Feargus O'Connor launched the Chartist Land Co-operative Society.
	May	Thomas Cooper released from prison. Publication of Disraeli's *Sybil: Or, The Two Nations.*
	Autumn	Onset of the Irish Famine.
	September	The Society of Fraternal Democrats founded in London.
	December	Conference on the Land Plan at Manchester.
1846	January	Ernest Jones joined the Chartist movement.
	June	Repeal of the Corn Laws. Peel obliged to resign. Whig government formed with Lord John Russell as prime minister.
1847	January	The Irish Confederation formed by the Young Irelanders.
	April	Financial crisis.
	May	Passage of Factory (Ten Hour) Act. O'Connorville opened.
	July	General election, resulting in a victory for the Whigs. Feargus O'Connor elected MP for Nottingham.
	Autumn/winter	Increasing unemployment.
1848	February	Revolution in France and proclamation of the Second Republic. Publication in London of the *Communist Manifesto* in German.
	March	Protest in Trafalgar Square against the income tax turned into a demonstration for the Charter - with extensive rioting.
	April	Chartist Convention met in London.
	10 April	The Kennington Common demonstration for the presentation of the Third Petition to Parliament. The Petition was mocked by the House of Commons. Crown and Government Security (Treason-Felony) Act.
	May	Convening of the (Chartist) National Assembly, which implemented the New Plan of Organisation. Select Committee of the House of Commons appointed to investigate the Land Company. John Mitchel sentenced to fourteen years' transportation.

	12 June	Suppression of proposed mass meeting at Bishop Bonner's Fields, Bethnal Green, on Whit Monday.
	May-July	Disturbances throughout the country, resulting in extensive arrests and imprisonment of Chartist leaders, including Ernest Jones.
	July	Failed insurrection in Ireland.
	14-16 Aug.	Abortive risings in Ashton-under-Lyne and London
	August	Publication of the Select Committee's Reports on the Land Company.
1849	March	The National Parliamentary and Financial Reform Association founded.
	June	Motion for parliamentary reform, supported by O'Connor and Joseph Hume, defeated in the Commons (286 votes to 82).
		Harney launched the *Democratic Review.*
1850	January	Bronterre O'Brien founded the National Reform League.
		Open conflict between Harney and O'Connor, culminating in a majority for Harney and the Fraternal Democrats on the Chartist Executive.
	March	The defeated O'Connorites formed the National Charter League.
	June	Harney launched the *Red Republican.*
	July	Ernest Jones released from prison
	November	Publication of first English translation of the *Communist Manifesto* in the *Red Republican.*
1851	January	An O'Connorite Chartist Convention in Manchester, boycotted by the supporters of Harney, is an utter failure.
	February	Bill to dissolve the Land Company.
	April	Chartist Convention in London adopts a social programme.
	May	Ernest Jones starts *Notes to the People.*
		The Great Exhibition.
1852	April	Harney buys the *Northern Star*, changing the name to the *Star of Freedom.*
	May	Jones starts the *People's Paper.*
	June	O'Connor involved in a scuffle in the Commons, from which he is removed by the Sergeant at Arms. He is pronounced insane.
	November	The *Star of Freedom* folds.
1854	March	Jones summoned the 'Labour Parliament' at Manchester.
	c.May	Death of Dr Peter Murray M'Douall, who had recently emigrated to Australia.
1855	June	Abolition of duty on newspapers and pamphlets.
	August	Death of Feargus O'Connor.

1856	July	Return of John Frost to Britain, having received a free pardon.
1858	February	The final national Chartist Convention and end of the NCA.
	June	Abolition of the property qualification for MPs.
1864		Death of Bronterre O'Brien.
1867		The Second Reform Act enfranchised male householders in the boroughs.
1869		Death of Ernest Jones.
1872		The Ballot Act.
1877		Death of William Lovett.
1884		The Third Reform Act enfranchised male householders in the counties.
1892		Death of Thomas Cooper.
1897		Death of George Julian Harney, 'the Last of the Chartist Leaders'.

2. Bibliography of Chartist Studies

Classic and recent books relating to Chartism, many of which David Goodway refers to in his text. Publication is in London unless by a university press or otherwise indicated.

Allen, Joan, and Ashton, Owen R, eds, *Papers for the People: A Study of the Chartist Press*, Merlin Press, 2005

Ashton, Owen, Fyson, Robert, and Roberts, Stephen, eds, *The Chartist Legacy*, Rendlesham: Merlin Press, 1999

Ashton, Owen, Fyson, Robert, and Roberts, Stephen, eds, *The Chartist Movement: A New Annotated Bibliography*, Mansell, 1995

Ashton, Owen R, and Pickering, Paul A, *Friends of the People: 'Uneasy' Radicals in the Age of the Chartists*, Merlin Press, 2002

Black, Frank Gees, and Black, Renee Métivier, eds, *The Harney Papers*, Assen: Van Gorcum, 1969

Briggs, Asa, *Chartism*, Stroud: Sutton, 1998

Briggs, Asa, ed, *Chartist Studies*, Macmillan, 1959

Challinor, Raymond, *A Radical Lawyer in Victorian England: W P Roberts and the Struggle for Workers' Rights*, I B Tauris, 1990

Challinor, Raymond, and Ripley, Brian, *The Miners' Association: A Trade Union in the Age of the Chartists*, Lawrence & Wishart, 1968

Charlton, John, *The Chartists: The First National Workers' Movement*, Pluto Press, 1997

Chase, Malcolm, *Chartism: A New History*, Manchester University Press, 2007

Cole, G D H, *Chartist Portraits*, Macmillan, 1941

Epstein, James, *The Lion of Freedom: Feargus O'Connor and the Chartist Movement, 1832-1842*, Croom Helm, 1982

Epstein, James, and Thompson, Dorothy, eds, *The Chartist Experience: Studies in Working-Class Radicalism and Culture, 1830-1860*, London and Basingstoke: Macmillan, 1982

Finn, Margot C, *After Chartism: Class and Nation in English Radical Politics 1848-1874*, Cambridge University Press, 2004

Fraser, W Hamish, *Chartism in Scotland*, Pontypool: Merlin Press, 2010

Fraser, W Hamish, *Dr John Taylor, Chartist: Ayrshire Revolutionary*, Ayr: Ayrshire Archaeological and Natural History Society, 2006

Gammage, R G, *History of the Chartist Movement, 1837-1854*, New York: Augustus M. Kelley, 1969 (first published 1894)

Hall, Robert G, *Voices of the People: Democracy and Chartist Political Identity, 1830-1870*, Monmouth: Merlin Press, 2007

Goodway, David, *London Chartism: 1838-1848*, Cambridge University Press, 1982

Hadfield, Alice Mary, *The Chartist Land Company*, Newton Abbot: David & Charles, 1970

Harrison, J F C, and Thompson, Dorothy, *Bibliography of the Chartist Movement, 1837-1976*, Hassocks: Harvester Press, 1978

Jenkins, Mick, *The General Strike of 1842*, Lawrence & Wishart, 1980

Jones, David, *Chartism and the Chartists*, Allen Lane, 1975

Jones, David J V, *The Last Rising: The Newport Insurrection of 1839*, Oxford; Clarendon Press, 1999

Kovalev, Y V, ed, *An Anthology of Chartist Literature*, Moscow, 1956

Mather, F.C., *Chartism*, Historical Association, 1965

Mather, F.C., *Public Order in the Age of the Chartists*, Manchester University Press, 1959

Peacock, A J, *Bradford Chartism, 1838-1840*, York: St Anthony's Press, 1969

Pickering, Paul A, *Feargus O'Connor: A Political Life*, Monmouth: Merlin Press, 2008

Pickering, Paul A, *Chartism and the Chartists in Manchester and Salford*, Basingstoke: Macmillan, 1995

Plummer, Alfred, *Bronterre: A Political Biography of Bronterre O'Brien, 1804-1864*, Allen & Unwin, 1971

Prothero, I J, *Artisans and Politics in Early Nineteenth-Century London: John Gast and His Times*, Folkestone: Dawson, 1979

Roberts, Stephen, *The Chartist Prisoners: The Radical Lives of Thomas Cooper (1805-1892) and Arthur O'Neill (1819-1896)*, Bern and Oxford: Peter Lang, 2008

Roberts, Stephen, *Radical Politicians and Poets in Early Victorian Britain: The Voices of Six Chartist Leaders*, Lampeter: Edwin Mellen Press, 1993

Roberts, Stephen, and Thompson, Dorothy, *Images of Chartism*, Rendlesham: Merlin Press, 1998

Rothstein, Theodore, *From Chartism to Labourism: Historical Sketches of the English Working Class Movement*, Lawrence & Wishart, 1983 (first published 1929)

Royle, Edward, *Chartism*, Longman, 1996

Sanders, Mike, *The Poetry of Chartism: Aesthetics, Politics, History*, Cambridge University Press, 2009

Saville, John, *1848: The British State and the Chartist Movement*, Cambridge University Press, 1987

Saville, John, *Ernest Jones: Chartist*, Lawrence & Wishart, 1952

Schoyen, A. R., *The Chartist Challenge: A Portrait of George Julian Harney*, Heinemann, 1958

Taylor, Miles, *Ernest Jones, Chartism, and the Romance of Politics, 1819-1869*, Oxford University Press, 2003

Thompson, Dorothy, ed, *The Early Chartists*, London and Basingstoke: Macmillan, 1971

Thompson, Dorothy, *The Chartists: Popular Politics in the Industrial Revolution*, New York: Pantheon Books, 1984

Vincent, David, ed, *Testaments of Radicalism: Memoirs of Working Class Politicians 1790-1885*, Europa Publications, 1977

Wilks, Ivor G, *South Wales and the Rising of 1839: Class Struggle as Armed Struggle*, Croom Helm, 1984

Feargus O' Connor
from *Chartism and Reform* - Labour History MSS

The National Convention - 1839 - British Coffee House
Chartism & Reform (bound volume: Labour History MSS)

The Socialist History Society

The Socialist History Society was founded in 1992 and includes many leading Socialist and labour historians, academic and amateur researchers, in Britain and overseas. The SHS holds regular events, public meetings and seminars, and contributes to current historical debates and controversies. We produce a range of publications, including the journal *Socialist History* and a regular Newsletter.

The SHS is the successor to the Communist Party History Group, which was established in 1946 and is now totally independent of all political parties and groups. We are engaged in and seek to encourage historical studies from a Marxist and broadly-defined left perspective. We are interested in all aspects of human history from the earliest social formations to the present day and aim for an international approach.

We are particularly interested in the various struggles of labour, of women, of progressive campaigns and peace movements around the world, as well as the history of colonial peoples, black people, and all oppressed communities seeking justice, human dignity and liberation.

Each year we produce two issues of our journal *Socialist History,* one or two historical pamphlets in our *Occasional Publications* series, and frequent members' Newsletters. We hold public lectures and seminars mainly in London. In addition, we hold special conferences, book launches and joint events with other friendly groups.

Join the Socialist History Society today!
Members receive all our serial publications for the year at no extra cost and regular mailings about our activities. Members can vote at our AGM and seek election to positions on the committee, and are encouraged to participate in other society activities.

Annual membership fees for 2013 (renewable every January):

Full UK	£25.00
Concessionary UK	£18.00
Europe full	£30.00
Europe concessionary	£24.00
Rest of world full	£35.00
Rest of world concessionary	£29.00

For details of institutional subscriptions, please e-mail the Treasurer on francis@socialisthistorysociety.co.uk.

To join the society for 2013, please send your name and address plus a cheque/PO payable to **Socialist History Society** to: SHS, 50 Elmfield Road, Balham, London SW17 8AL. You can also pay online.
Visit our websites on www.socialisthistorysociety.co.uk and www.socialist-history-journal.org.uk.

Other SHS Occasional Publications for sale

31 Marilyn J Boxer and John S Partington (eds), *Clara Zetkin: National and International Contexts*, £7.00

30 Richard Hart, *Caribbean Workers' Struggles*, £6.00

29 Willie Thompson, *Setting an Agenda, Thomson, Dobb, Hill and the Communist Party Historians*, £3.00

28 Deborah Lavin, *Bradlaugh contra Marx. Radicalism versus Socialism in the First International*, £4.00

27 David Howell, Dianne Kirby and Kevin Morgan (eds), *John Saville: Commitment and History. Themes from the life and work of a socialist historian*, £14.99

25 Francis King, *The Narodniks in the Russian Revolution: Russia's Socialist-Revolutionaries in 1917*, £5.00

24 Paul Auerbach, Willie Thompson, *Is there No Alternative? Historical Problems of Socialist Economic Strategies*, £2.50

23 Jim Riordan, *The last British Comrade trained in Moscow: the Higher Party School 1961 - 1963* , £2.50

22 Gavin Bowd, *Comintern Cadre: The Passion of Allan Eaglesham*, £2.50

21 Lionel Munby, D Huw Owen, James Scannell, *Local History since 1945: England, Wales and Ireland*, £3.00

19 W Raymond Powell, *Keir Hardie in West Ham: "A Constituency with a Past"*, £2.50

17 Linda Colley, *Another Making of the English Working Class: The Lash and the Imperial Soldiery*, £2.00

14 Victor Kiernan, *Twenty Years of Europe: The Engels-Lafargue Correspondence*, £2.75

12 Jim Fyrth, *An Indian Landscape 1944-1946*, £5.50

To order these and other SHS Occasional Publications online, please visit http://www.socialisthistorysociety.co.uk/shop.htm. These pamphlets can also be ordered by post within the UK — please send a cheque for the requisite amount (post free) payable to **Socialist History Society**, together with your name and address, to

SHS
50 Elmfield Road
London
SW17 8AL